PYTHON ANALYSIS:

LEARN THE PRICIPLES OF DATA ANALYSIS AND RAISE YOUR PROGRAMMING IQ. IMPROVE YOUR MACHINE LEARNING EXPERIENCE AND BECOME A SKILLED PROGRAMMER BY LEARNING 10+ CODING SECRETS

Robert Campbell

Table of Contents

Introduction

The Python programming language is characterized by an easy to learn and intuitive syntax, making it one of the most widely used and preferred programming languages across the world. According to the TIOBE index, Python is ranked as the third popularly used language in 2019. This ranking takes its usage up even further, implying a two percent increase from the previous year.

Python's popularity can also be traced to the high readability of its syntax and simplicity of use. Readability comes in terms of the syntax being written in clean, regular English. This property makes the program less daunting to code in and allows programmers to pay attention to the business at hand instead of trying to keep up with and remember all the details of the language.

How Python Started

Python programming began at the fingertips of a Dutch programmer, name of Guido Van Rossum. He wrote the program sometime in the latter period of the '80s as a hobby project. Since its release to the public, Python has grown and evolved over time to be one of the most acclaimed, polished, and consistent languages in the world of computer programming.

According to Van Rossum, the conception of Python can be traced to a Christmas weekend in December 1989. He had begun working on his hobby project in his free time to develop an interpreter language—a successor to the ABC programming language to which Van Rossum helped develop. However, when the entire process of development came to an end, Python emerged as nothing short of a complete programming language in itself. Given its somewhat already weird history, the name "Python" draws even more questions to the identity of the programming language. Van Rossum had the Unix and C hackers as the target audience of his program, but more importantly, he was especially keen on the then famous TV sitcom—The Monty

Python's Flying Circus. Van Rossum explained that he found the name "Python" not only suitable to his taste but appealing to his target audience, so he ran with it.

Properties of Python Programming Language

Python is a dynamically and implicitly typed language in itself, so you are not required to declare variables while coding. The datatypes in Python are enforced, and its variables are sensitive to case. As a result, VALUE and value are processed as two distinct variable types. Furthermore, there are no set out characters used in terminating statements or commands. Every block of code is specified with an indentation. As such, at the beginning of a block of code, an indent is introduced, and a de-dent is used at the end. Statements that require a level of indentation are terminated using a colon (:). To add comments, the hash (#) is used in each line. For multiple line strings, they are used in multi-line comments. To assign values to variables, the equal to (=) is used, while the double equal to (==) signs are used in testing for equality. Increment and decrement can be performed on values using the operators (+=) and (-=), respectively, with the amount placed on the right-hand side of the operator. Such operations can be performed on strings and several other data types.

What is Data Analysis

Data analysis is basically the use of data analytics tools and methods in respect to achieving business goals.

It is a process in which we; scrutinize, transform and sort unprocessed data in order to generate useful information: this process permits evaluation of data through logical and analytical reasoning.

During data analytics, data is generally collected and inspected. It has several uses. While, analyzing data is: Defining, investigation, purification, removing Na values and other outliers in the data and transforming it to produce useful results. To perform data analysis, one need to know the tools in order to take prerequisite action on data awareness of Python, R, SAS, Apache Spark, Tableau Public, Excel, etc. and more. One needs to be keen on tools for data analysis as KNIME, Open Refine.

Data analysis process also comes under data analytics. This involves,

Data collecting.

Data polishing.

Analysis of data.

Data Interpretation.

The final process embraces you with what the data wishes said.

While figuring out the next step next, in regard to marketing, we use analytics since they insure predicting later numbers. However, in regard to data analysis, the process is performed on the final set of data to comprehend prior engagements. Critically, data analytics and data analysis are a necessity to understanding data and how useful it is when comprehending the later demands. They are used to perform data analysis with an overview of the past.

The two basic principles in analyzing data are; Interpolation and extrapolation. Interpolation is taking a look at the data, based on current data; determine past. Especially, this can be useful when performing market analysis and the like. However, extrapolation is taking the current data and making a brave guess as to how it will be in the coming years. It is extensively used of the two as institutions are highly concerned with the future than the past.

These two methods will be wide in your career whence ensuring you know both of them places one at where programming converges. Data usage has rapidly grown in the recent past as huge amount of data gets gathered in the companies. The data is/or might be related to business customers and application users, visitors or even stakeholders. The data is divided and processed to comprehend, decode, and analyze patterns. Data analytics in itself comprises of various skills and tools. Engaging in quantitative and qualitative techniques for gathering data aims for an outcome that can be maximized for graded efficiency, risk reduction, production increment and continued growth of businesses. These methods vary from company to company depending on their demands.

Specifically, data analysis is a special idea; making a tool that uses technologies as tableau public, KNIME, Open Refine and Rapid Miner among others. These tools are used for exploratory analysis hence this gives insight from the available data by; cleaning, using, transforming, modeling and visualizing the data to provide the outcome.

Necessary skills for becoming a data scientist

These are some skills required to become a data scientist.

1. Education: getting a degree in these courses equips you with the necessary skills for processing and analyzing a large amount of data. Though, getting the degree course, do not guarantee that you are through.

The variety of skills you have learned doing your degree program helps to move into data science.

A research paper can clearly and easily destroy the world of data science. Keeping this in mind, ensure a constancy to keep in touch with the data analytics world. This can enable you perform ahead of your colleagues since you will be familiar with the principles and techniques.

2. R Programming: R is majorly used for data science as it is tailored for the data science demands. R is also used to solve all problems faced in data science.

R is generally less useful than other languages in general-purpose programming situations. It's good for data analytics, not usable for anything else comparable important. For a first language, this makes it not ideal, you'll find that even when able to analyze the data, making programs that will be able to actually use it will be a hard nut to crack. In the long run, one wants to focus on making programs that can reliably use data while patronizing the implications on your data.

3. Python coding: This is a great choice for the data scientists accompanied by Java, Perl, C++ and C. 40% of the users prefer Python as their primary programming language option according to a survey conducted by O'Reilly.

4. Using Hadoop Platform: It is a huge and strong opportunity to be experienced in Pig or Hive. Being familiar with various cloud tools such as Amazon S3 gives you a high definition.

5. SQL DB/Coding: SQL is a Structured Query Language known popularly as a programming language which can be useful for conducting out various operations like addition, deletion, and extraction of data from the DB. When you utilize it for querying a DB it will provide insight.

6. Apache Spark: This is one of the big and most popular data technologies available. Similar to Hadoop, Apache Spark is a big data

computation framework. The use of Apache Spark is more advantageous considering that it is faster than Hadoop.

7. AI and Machine Learning: Machine learning and related techniques such as reinforcement learning, neural networks and adversarial learning, is an area which many data scientists out there are not proficient in.

8. Data Visualization: Regularly, in most cases huge amount of data generated in businesses worldwide. Usually, the large data should be decoded into the right readable format.

9. Data that is not structured: Basically, the unformed data is all the system less contents that do not suit in the DB tables.

10. Intellectually curious nature: Owing to the fact that the field of data science is growing rapidly, a data scientist, should and must be able to enquire questions in the field. Since the scientists spend most of their time gathering and sorting data

11. Business understanding: You are expected to contain great comprehending of your industry, knowing the various business problems facing your institution.

12. Communication Skills: People who can perfectly and coherently read and interpret technical things to non-technical teams like the sales and marketing department. These are the great minded data analysts that organizations are searching. This can yield huge growth in businesses by impacting positively through provision of quality services.

13. Teamwork: You need to be able to work freely and as team with the rest in a company. Working with other company officials is a tool to develop and strategize development plans. You can work with the corporate communication department for marketing purposes. In order to create good products, you will interact with mangers and designers

Python Libraries for Data Analysis

The program is assistance to the developers for creation lstandalone PC games and mobiles. With its huge libraries of 137000, Python assist in many ways.

Some certification programs on social media platforms like blogs and videos are very useful in training. You can find blogs, videos, and other resources online as well. Most critical tasks that need important information in order to be done effectively by the data scientists will require guide information to make important decisions concerning the running of business operations and other critical tasks.

1. NumPy: For data scientists and developers, it is one of the first options for those who know technologies involved in data related things. This Python package is used for performing scientific computations is registered under the BSD license.

2. Theano: Theano is a very helpful library in pythhelps data scientists to create huge several dimensions arrays in conjunction with computing tasks. Similarly, it is same as TensorFlow only that it is not that effective efficiently. It's primarily involved in the parallel and tasks in relation with distributed computing.

3. Keras: Keras is among the empowering libraries in python. It allows for interaction higher-level neural network. Universally, permits different execution and blends over CPU and GPU.

It ensures and awards a user-friendly surrounding thus, decreasing the force needed for cognitive loads and making available results that need to be achieved by the use of simple APIs.

4. PyTorch: This is among the biggest machine learning libraries in python availed to data scientists, other researchers and analysts. This assists them with computational graph designs characterized by constant change. We are talking about quick tensor computation accelerated via GPU and other hard techniques available.

5. SciPy: This Python library is used by data scientists, developers and also researchers. Occasionally, one may be bewildered between, SciPy

stack with the library. Basically, SciPy gives you effectiveness, combination, linear algebra computation packages and also statistics.

6. Pandas: PANDAS is the Python Data Analysis Library. Being a wide not closed library source, it is used for providing analysis tools and data structures which are high-performance. On the NumPy package, in which its main data structure is Data Frame PANDAS is created.

7. PyBrain: this contains various algorithms created and obtained for; supervised and unsupervised learning, neural network and evolution.

8. SciKit-Learn: mainly, this tool is simply useful for tasks such data analyzing and data mining. It is an open source type of tool which can be used recycled and used by all in dynamic contexts, it is also licensed under BSD

9. Matplotlib: This Python library is usually known and familiar among data scientists. It is uses for 2D plotting for tailoring dynamic figures in multiple formats around the structures respectively.

10. TensorFlow: through the use of empowered ML algorithms, it is used for computing the data low graphs mainly. The more importantly, the library was tailored to accomplish the neural network work. High demands for training

11. Seaborn: This was tailored for the purpose visualizing complex statistical models. It comes with the ability and capability to deliver accurate graphs such as heat maps. Seaborn is created using the idea of the Matplotlib. Due to this, it is highly reliant on the Matplotli.

12. Bokeh: It is created for the purpose of interactive plots. This is one of the various visual purpose libraries. In conjunction with Seaborn, sit is also designed using the Matplotlib concept.

13. Plotly: this is one of the vast used and well known web based structure. This framework uses a various varieties of API supported by the multiple programming languages such as Python, to offer visualization models of design.

14. NLTK: This is the short form for Natural Language Toolkit. Initially, it was designed to support teaching models used in AI and linguistic models: This is alongside NLP enabled research such as the cognitive theory. It enables achieving of natural language processing tasks.

15. Gensim: Through the use of implemented range of tools, this Python-based open source library allows topic modeling and space vector computation. It is compatible with the big test and creates a well-organized t operation and in-memory processing.

16. Scrapy: This python library is accountable for retrieving structured data out of web applications and for crawling on the programs. Similarly, known as spider bots, scrapy is a Python written open source library created for scraping.

17. Statsmodels: this is another Python library, accountable for giving exploration modules. Statsmodels mainly uses multiple methods for carrying out statistical analysis and assertions.

18. Kivy: The open source library licensed under MIT. It is highly useful in the creation of mobile apps accompanied by multi-touch applications. This Python library is accountable for supplying of a natural user interface that can effectively be accessed through Linux, Android and even windows.

19. PyQt: This is a free application which is licensed under the General Public License (GNU). It is having executed as the Python plugin. The Python connecting toolkit is being used as a cross-platform GUI.

20. OpenCV: This open source Intel created platform is licensed with BSD. It is tailored for driving the growth of real-time computation application development.

Python Crash Course

One of the best coding languages that you are able to work with when you want to start handling your own data science project is the Python language. This is a fantastic language that is able to take on all of the work that you want to do with data science and has the power that is needed to help create some great machine learning algorithms. With that said, it is still a great option for beginners because it has been designed to work with those who have never done programming before. While you can choose to work with the R programming language as well, you will find that the Python language is one of the best options because of its ease of use and power that combines together.

The Statements

The first thing that we are going to take a moment to look through when it comes to our Python language is the keywords. This is going to focus on the lines or sentences that you would like to have the compiler show up on your screen. You will need to use some of the keywords that we will talk about soon, and then you can tell the compiler what statements to put up on the screen. If you would like to leave a message on the screen such as what we can do with the Hello, World! The program, you will need to use that as your statement, and the print keyword, so the complier knows how to behave.

The Python Operators

We can also take some time to look at what is known as the Python operators. These are often going to get ignored when it comes time to write out codes because they don't seem like they are that important. But if you skip out on writing them, they are going to really make it so that your code will not work the way that you would like. There are a number of different types of Python operators that we are able to focus on, so making sure that you know what each kind is all about, and when to add these into your code, will make a world of difference as well.

The Keywords

The keywords are another important part of our Python code that we need to take a look at. These are going to be the words that we need to reserve because they are responsible for giving the compiler the instructions or the commands that you would like for it to use. These key words ensure that the code is going to perform the way that you would like it to the whole time.

These keywords need to be reserved, so make sure that you are not using them in the wrong places. If you do not use these keywords in the right manner, or you don't put them in the right place, then the compiler is going to end up with some issues understanding what you would like it to do, and you will not be able to get the results that you want. Make sure to learn the important keywords that come with the Python language and learn how to put them in the right spot of your code to get the best results with it.

Working with Comments

As we work with the Python coding, there are going to be times when we need to spend our time working with something that is known as a comment. This is going to be one of the best things that we are able to do in order to make sure that we can name a part of the code, or when we want to leave a little note for yourself or for another programmer, then you are going to need to work with some of the comments as well.

These comments are going to be a great option to work with. They are going to allow you to really leave a nice message in the code, and the compiler will know that it should just skip over that part of the code, and not read through it at all. It is as simple as that and can save you a lot of hassle and work inside of any code you are doing.

So, any time that you would like to write out a comment inside of your Python code, you just need to use the # symbol, and then the compiler will know that it is supposed to skip over that part of the code and not read it. We are able to add in as many of these comments as we would like into the code. Just remember to keep these to the number that is necessary, rather than going overboard with this, because it ensures that we are going to keep the code looking as nice and clean as possible.

The Python Class

You can store anything that you want inside a class that you design, but you must ensure that things that are similar end up in the same class. The items don't have to be identical to each other, but when someone takes a look at the class that you worked on, they need to be able to see that those objects belong together and make sense to be together.

For example, you don't have to just put cars into the same class, but you could have different vehicles in the same class. You could have items that are considered food. You can even have items that are all the same color. You get some freedom when creating the classes and storing objects in those classes, but when another programmer looks at the code, they should be able to figure out what the objects inside that class are about and those objects should share something in common.

Classes are very important when it comes to writing out your code. These are going to hold onto the various objects that you write in the code and can ensure that everything is stored properly. They will also make it easier for you to call out the different parts of your code when you need them for execution.

How to Name Your Identifiers

Inside the Python language, there are going to be a number of identifiers that we need to spend some time on. Each of these identifiers is going to be important, and they are going to make a big difference in some of the different parts of the code that you are able to work with. They are going to come to us under a lot of different names, but you will find that they are going to follow the same kinds of rules when it comes to naming them, and that can make it a lot easier for a beginner to work with as well.

To start with, you can use a lot of different types of characters in order to handle the naming of the identifiers that you would like to work with. You are able to use any letter of the alphabet that you would like, including uppercase and lowercase, and any combination of the two that you would like. Using numbers and the underscore symbol is just fine in this process as well.

With this in mind, there are going to be a few rules that you have to remember when it comes to naming your identifiers. For example, you are not able to start out a name with the underscore symbol or with a number. So, writing something like 3puppies or _threepuppies would not work. But you can do it with something like threepuppies for the name. A programmer also won't be able to add in spaces between the names either. You can write out threepuppies or three_puppies if you would like, but do not add the space between the two of them.

In addition to some of these rules, we need to spend some time looking at one other rule that is important to remember. Pick out a name for your identifier that is easy to remember and makes sense for that part of the code. This is going to ensure that you are able to understand the name and that you will be able to remember it later on when you need to call it up again.

Python Functions

Another topic that we are going to take a quick look at here as we work with the Python language is the idea of the Python functions. These are going to be a set of expressions that can also be statements inside of your code as well. You can have the choice to give them a name or let them remain anonymous. They are often the first-class objects that we are able to explore as well, meaning that your restrictions on how to work with them will be lower than we will find with other class objects.

Now, these functions are very diversified and there are many attributes that you can use when you try to create and bring up those functions. Some of the choices that you have with these functions include:

__doc__: This is going to return the docstring of the function that you are requesting.

Func_default: This one is going to return a tuple of the values of your default argument.

Func_globals: This one will return a reference that points to the dictionary holding the global variables for that function.

Func_dict: This one is responsible for returning the namespace that will support the attributes for all your arbitrary functions.

Func_closure: This will return to you a tuple of all the cells that hold the bindings for the free variables inside of the function.

There are different things that you can do with your functions, such as passing it as an argument over to one of your other functions if you need it. Any function that is able to take on a new one as the argument will be considered the higher-order function in the code. These are good to learn because they are important to your code as you move.

The Importance of Variables

While we are working with the Python programming language, we are going to run across sometimes when we need to work with the Python variables. These are going to be spaces in the memory of our computer that are able to hold spaces for the different values that are in any code that we are writing. This makes it easier for the code to pull up what is needed at the right times, simply by calling up the variable that we ask for as well.

Assigning a value to a variable is a pretty easy process. We just need to name the variable and then use the equal sign in order to get it all done. As long as the equal sign is in between the two, your compiler is going to know which value is going to be assigned back to which variable that is in the system. And if you would like to assign more than one value to a single variable, you would just need to make sure that there is an equal sign that falls in between all of that as well.

As we can see with some of the different parts that we have just looked through in this guidebook, learning how to work with the Python coding language is a great option to work with as well. Even if you have never spent any time working with coding in the past, and you are looking to just get into it in order to learn how to work with data science and one of these projects for your company.

Data Munging

The Process

Data munging comes after uploading the data, however at the moment that raw data cannot be used for any kind of analysis. Data can be chaotic, and filled with senseless information or gaps. This is why, as an aspiring data scientist, you solve this problem with the use of Python data structures that will turn this data into a data set that contains variables. You will need these data sets when working with any kind of statistical or machine learning analysis. Data munging might not be the most exciting phase in data science, but it is the foundation for your project and much needed to extract the valuable data you seek to obtain.

In the next phase, once you observe the data you obtain, you will begin to create a hypothesis that will require testing. You will examine variables graphically, and come up with new variables. You will use various data science methodologies such as machine learning or graph analysis in order to establish the most effective variables and their parameters. In other words, in this phase you process all the data you obtain from the previous phase and you create a model from it. You will undoubtedly realize in your testing that corrections are needed and you will return to the data munging phase to try something else. It's important to keep in mind that most of the time, the solution for your hypothesis will be nothing like the actual solution you will have at the end of a successful project. This is why you cannot work purely theoretically. A good data scientist is required to prototype a large variety of potential solutions and put them all to the test until the best course of action is revealed.

One of the most essential parts of the data science process is visualizing the results through tables, charts, and plots. In data science, this is referred to as "OSEMN", which stands for "Obtain, Scrub, Explore, Model, Interpret". While this abbreviation doesn't entirely illustrate the process behind data science, it captures the most important stages you should be aware of as an aspiring data scientist. Just keep in mind that data munging will often take the majority of your efforts when working on a project.

Importing Datasets with pandas

We need pandas to first start by loading the tabular data, such as spreadsheets and databases, from any files. This tool is great because it will create a data structure where every row will be indexed, variables kept separate by delimiters, data can be converted, and more.

You can explore the object's content just to see how it looks for now by typing the following line:

In: iris.head()

As you can see, we aren't using any parameters with these commands, so what you should get is a table with only the first 5 rows, because that's the default if there are no arguments. However, if you want a certain number of rows to be displayed, simply type the instruction like this:

iris.head(3)

Now you should see the first three rows instead. Next, let's access the column names by typing:

In: iris.columns

Out: Index(['sepal_length', 'sepal_width', 'petal_length',

'petal_width', 'target'], dtype='object')

The result of this will be a pandas index of the column names that looks like a list. Let's extract the target column. You can do it like this:

In: Y = iris['target']

Y

Out:

0Iris-setosa

1Iris -setosa

2Iris -setosa

3Iris -setosa

...

149Iris-virginica

Name: target, dtype: object

For now it's important only to understand that Y is a pandas series. That means it is similar to an array, but in this case it's one directional. Another thing that we notice in this example is that the pandas Index class is just like a dictionary index. Now let's type the following:

In: X = iris[['sepal_length', 'sepal_width']]

All we did now was asking for a list of columns by index. By doing so, we received a pandas dataframe as the result. In the first example, we received a one dimensional pandas series. Now we have a matrix instead, because we requested multiple columns. What's a matrix? If your basic math is a bit rusty, you should know that it is an array of numbers that are arranged in rows and columns.

Next, we want to have the dimensions of the dataset:

In: print (X.shape)

Out: (150, 2)

In: print (Y.shape)

Out: (150,)

What we have now is a tuple. We can now see the size of the array in both dimensions. Now that you know the basics of this process, let's move on to basic preprocessing.

Preprocessing Data with pandas

The next step after learning how to load datasets is to get accustomed to the data preprocessing routines. Let's say we want to apply a function to a certain section of rows. To achieve this, we need a mask. What's a mask? It's a series of true or false values (Boolean) that we need to tell when a certain line is selected. As always, let's examine an example because reading theory can be dry and confusing.

In: mask_feature = iris['sepal_length'] > 6.0

In: mask_feature

0False

1False

...

146True

147True

148True

149False

In this example we're trying to select all the lines of our "iris" dataset that have the value of "sepal length" larger than 6. You can clearly see the observations that are either true or false, and therefore know the ones that fit our query. Now let's use a mask in order to change our "iris-virginica" target with a new label. Type:

In: mask_target = iris['target'] == 'Iris-virginica'

In: iris.loc[mask_target, 'target'] = 'New label'

All "Iris-virginica" labels will now be shown as "New label" instead. We are using the "loc()" method to access this data with row and column indexes. Next, let's take a look at the new label list in the "target" column. Type:

In: iris['target'].unique()

Out: array(['Iris-setosa', 'Iris-versicolor', 'New label'],   dtype=object)

In this example we are using the "unique" method to examine the new list. Next we can check the statistics by grouping every column. Let's see this in action first, and then discuss how it works. Type:

In: grouped_targets_mean = iris.groupby(['target']).mean()

grouped_targets_mean

Out:

In: grouped_targets_var = iris.groupby(['target']).var()

grouped_targets_var

Out:

We start by grouping each column with the "groupby" method. If you are a bit familiar with SQL, it's worth noting that this works similarly to the "GROUP BY" instruction. Next, we use the "mean" method, which computes the average of the values. This is an aggregate method that can be applied to one or several columns. Then we can have several other pandas methods such as "var" which stands for the variance, "sum" for the summation, "count" for the number of rows, and more. Keep in mind that the result you are looking at is still a data frame. That means that you can link as many operations as you want. In our example we are using the "groupby" method to group the observations by label and then check what the difference is between the values and variances for each of our groups.

Now let's assume the dataset contains a time series. What's a time series, you ask? In data science, sometimes we have to analyze a series of data points that are graphed in a certain chronological order. In other words, it is a sequence of the equally spaced points in time. Time series are used often in statistics, for weather forecasting, and for counting sunspots. Often, these datasets have really noisy data points, so we have to use a "rolling" operation, like this:

In: smooth_time_series = pd.rolling_mean(time_series, 5)

Now let's explore pandas "apply" method that has many uses due to its ability to perform programmatically operations on rows and columns. Let's see this in action by counting the number of non-zero elements that exist in each line.

In: iris.apply(np.count_nonzero, axis=1).head()

Out:05

15

25

35

45

dtype: int64

Lastly, let's use the "applymap" method for element level operations. In the next example, we are going to assume we want the length of the string representation of each cell. Type:

In: iris.applymap(lambda el:len(str(el))).head()

To receive our value, we need to cast every individual cell to a string value. Once that is done, we can gain the value of the length.

Data Selection with pandas

The final section about working with pandas is data selection. Let's say you find yourself in a situation where your dataset has an index column, and you need to import it and then manipulate it. To visualize this, let's say we have a dataset with an index from 100. Here's how it would look:

n,val1,val2,val3

100,10,10,C

101,10,20,C

102,10,30,B

103,10,40,B

104,10,50,A

So the index of row 0 is 100. If you import such a file, you will have an index column like in our case labeled as "n". There's nothing really wrong with it, however you might use the index column by mistake, so you should separate it instead in order to prevent such errors from happening. To avoid possible issues and errors, all you need to do is mention that "n" is an index column. Here's how to do it:

In: dataset = pd.read_csv('a_selection_example_1.csv',

index_col=0) dataset

Out:

Your index column should now be separate. Now let's access the value inside any cell. There's more than one way to do that. You can simply target it by mentioning the column and line. Let's assume we want to obtain "Val3" from the 5th line, which is marked by an index of 104.

In: dataset['val3'][104]

Out: 'A'

Keep in mind that this isn't a matrix, even though it might look like one. Make sure to specify the column first, and then the row in order to extract the value from the cell you want.

Categorical and Numerical Data

Numerical data is quite self-explanatory, as it deals with any data expressed in numbers, such as temperature or sums of money.

Categorical data, on the other hand, is expressed by a value that can't be measured. A great example of this type of data, which is sometimes referred to as nominal data, is the weather, which holds values such as sunny, partially cloudy, and so on. Basically, data to which you cannot apply equal to, greater than, or less than operators is nominal data. Other examples of this data include products you purchase from an online store, computer IDs, IP addresses, etc. Booleans are the one thing that is needed to work with both categorical and numerical data. They can even be used to encode categorical values as numerical values. Let's see an example:

Categorical_feature = sunnynumerical_features = [1, 0, 0, 0, 0]

Categorical_feature = foggynumerical _features = [0, 1, 0, 0, 0]

Categorical_feature = snowynumerical _features = [0, 0, 1, 0, 0]

Categorical_feature = rainynumerical _features = [0, 0, 0, 1, 0]

Categorical_feature = cloudynumerical _features = [0, 0, 0, 0, 1]

This turns the information into a map with 5 true or false statements for each categorical feature we listed. One of the numerical features (1) confirms the categorical feature, while the other four are o. Now let's turn this result into a dataframe that presents each categorical feature as a column and the numerical features next to that column. To achieve this you need to type the following code:

In: import pandas as pd

categorical_feature = pd.Series(['sunny', 'foggy', 'snowy', 'rainy', 'cloudy'])

mapping = pd.get_dummies(categorical_feature)

mapping

Out:

In data science, this is called binarization. We do not use one categorical feature with as many levels as we have. Instead, we create all the categorical features and assign two binary values to them. Next we can map the categorical values to a list of numerical values. This is how it would look:

In: mapping['sunny']

Out:

01.0

10.0

20.0

30.0

40.0

Name: sunny, dtype: float64

In: mapping['foggy']

Out:

00.0

11.0

20.0

30.0

40.0

Name: cloudy, dtype: float64

Why Data Preprocessing Is Important

What Is Data Preprcoessing?

Let's suppose that you are going through some of the log files of a website and analyzing these, hoping to find out which IP out of all the options the spammers are coming from.

Or you can use this to figure out which demographic on the website is leading to more sales.

An analysis has to be performed on the data with two important columns to provide answers to such questions and more.

These are going to include the number of hits that have been made to the website, and the IP address of the hit.

As we can imagine here, the log files that you are analyzing are not going to be structured, and they could contain a lot of textual information that is unstructured.

To keep this simple, preparing the log file to extract the data in the format that you require in order to analyze it can be the process known as data preparation.

Data preparation is a big part of the whole data science process.

According to CrowdFlower, which is a provider of data enrichment platforms that data scientists can work with, it is seen that out of 80 data scientists, they will spend their day in the following:

60 percent of their time is spent on organizing and then cleaning the data they have collected.

19 percent is spent on collecting the sets of data that they want to use.

9 percent is used to mine the data that they have collected and prepared in order to draw the necessary patterns.

3 percent of their time will be spent doing any of the necessary training for the sets of data.

4 percent of the time is going to be spent trying to refine the algorithms that were created and working on getting them better at their jobs.

5 percent of the time is spent on some of the other tasks that are needed for this job.

As we can see from the statistics of the survey above, it helps us to see that most of the time for that data scientist is spent in preparing the data, which means they have to spend a good deal of time organizing, cleaning, and collecting, before they are even able to start on the process of analyzing the data.

The amount of time that you actually will spend on preparing the data for a specific problem with the analysis is going to depend directly on the health of the data.

If there are a lot of errors, missing parts, and duplicate values, then this is a process that will take a lot longer.

Why Do I Need Data Preprocessing?

One question that a lot of people have when it is time to work on the process of data preparation is why they need to do it in the first place.

It may seem to someone who is just getting started in this field that collecting the data and getting it all as organized as possible would be the best steps to take, and then they can go on to making their own model.

But there are a few different reasons why data preparation will be so important to this process, and they will include the following:

The set of data that you are working with could contain a few discrepancies in the codes or the names that you are using.

The set of data that you are working with could contain a lot of outliers or some errors that mess with the results.

The set of data that you are working with will lack your attributes of interest to help with the analysis.

The set of data that you want to explore is not going to be qualitative, but it is going to be quantitative.

These are not the same things, and often having more quality is going to be the most important.

Each of these things has the potential to really mess up the model that you are working on and could get you results or predictions that are not as accurate as you would like.

Taking the time to prepare your data and get it clean and ready to go can solve this issue and will ensure that your data is going to be more than ready to use in no time.

What Are the Steps for Data Preprocessing?

At this point, we need to take some time to look at some of the steps that are needed to handle the data preparation for data mining.

The first step is to clean the data.

This is one of the first and most important steps to handling the data and getting it prepared.

We need to go through and correct any of the data that is inconsistent by filling out some of the values that are missing and then smoothing out the outliers and any data that is making a lot of noise and influencing the analysis in a negative manner.

There is the possibility that we end up with many rows in our set of data that do not have a value for the attributes of interest, or they could be inconsistent data that is there as well.

In some cases, there are records that have been duplicated or some other random error that shows up.

We need to tackle all of these issues with the data quality as quickly as possible in order to get a model at the end that provides us with an honest and reliable prediction.

There are a few methods that we can use to handle some of the missing values.

The method that is chosen is going to be dependent on the requirement either by ignoring the tuple or filling in some of the missing values with the mean value of the attribute.

This can be done with the help of the global constant or with some of the other Python machine learning techniques, including the Bayesian formulae or a decision tree.

We can also take some time to tackle the noisy data when needed.

It is possible to handle this in a manual manner.

Or there are several techniques of clustering or regression that can help us to handle this as well. You have to choose the one that is needed based on the data that you have.

The second step that we need to focus on here is going to be known as data integration.

This step is going to involve a few things like integrating the schema, resolving some of the conflicts of the data if any shows up, and even handling any of the redundancies that show up in the data that you are using.

Next on the list is going to be the idea of data transformation.

This step is going to be important because it will take the time to handle some of the noise that is found in your data.

This step is going to help us to take out that noise from the data so it will not cause the analysis you have to go wrong.

We can also see the steps of normalization, aggregation, and generalization showing up in this step as well.

We can then move on to the fourth step, which is going to be all about reducing the data.

a reduced representation of their set of data.

We want this set to be smaller in size than some of the others, but inclusive enough that it will provide us with some of the same analysis outcomes that we want.

This can be hard when we have a very large set of data, but there are a few reduction strategies for the data that we can apply.

Some of these are going to include the numerosity reduction, aggregation, data cube, and dimensionality reduction, and more, based on the requirements that you have.

And finally, the fifth step of this is going to be known as data discretization.

The set of data that you are working with will contain three types of attributes.

Some of the algorithms that you will choose to work with only handle the attributes that are categorical.

This step of data discretization can help someone in data science divide continuous attributes into intervals, and can also help reduce the size of the data.

This helps us to prepare it for analysis.

Take your time with this one to make sure that it all matches up and does some of the things that you are expecting.

Many of the methods and the techniques that you are able to use with this part of the process are going to be strong and can get a lot of the work with you.

But even with all of these tools, it is still considered an area of research, one that many scientists are going to explore more and hopefully come up with some new strategies and techniques that you can use to get it done.

Handling the Missing Data

It is common for data to become missing in many applications of data analysis.

One of the goals of working with the Pandas library here is that we want to make working with some of this missing data as easy and as painless as possible.

For example, all of the descriptive statistics that happen on the objects of Pandas exclude the missing data by default.

The way that this data is going to be represented in Pandas is going to have some problems, but it can be really useful for many of the users who decide to go with this kind of library.

For some of the numeric data that we may have to work with, the Pandas library is going to work with a floating-point value that is known as NaN, or not a number, to represent the data that is missing inside of our set of data.

In the Pandas library, we have adopted a convention that is used in the programming language of R in order to refer to the missing data.

This missing data is going to show up as NA, which means not available right now.

In the applications of statistics, NA data can either be data that doesn't exist at all, or that exists, but we are not going to be able to observe through problems with collecting the data.

When cleaning up the data to be analyzed, it is often important to do some of the analysis on the missing data itself to help identify the collection of the data and any problems or potential biases in the data that has been caused by the missing data.

There are also times when the data is going to have duplicates.

When you get information online or from other sets of data, it is possible that some of the results will be duplicated.

If this happens often, then there is going to be a mess with the insights and predictions that you get.

The data is going to lean towards the duplicates, and it will not work the way that you would like.

There are ways that you can work with the Pandas library in order to really improve this and make sure that the duplicates are eliminated or are at least limited at least a little bit.

There is so much that we are able to do when it comes to working with data preparation in order to complete the process of data mining and getting the results that we want in no time with our analysis.

Make sure to take some time on this part, as it can really make or break the system that we are trying to create.

If you do spend enough time on it, and ensure that the data is as organized and clean as possible, you are going to be happy with the results and ready to take on the rest of the process.

What is Data Wrangling?

During the import, you have to map the data headers in your export file to the values the email service recognizes. You have to set the rule of declaring "email ID" is the same as "email address" to avoid any data errors. After the import is complete, the customer details are saved in the email service database. This is a simple example of data wrangling. Here are some tools used for data wrangling:

The NumPy and SciPy Library

The first two libraries that we are going to explore here are going to be the NumPy, or Numeric and Scientific Computation, and the SciPy library. NumPy is a useful library to learn about because it is going to help us lay down some of the basic premises that are needed for any kind of scientific computing that we wish to do with Python. It is also going to be there to help us grab the functions that we need, many of which are precompiled and fast enough to help out with any and all mathematical and numerical routines.

In addition to some of the listed benefits that we have above, NumPy is also able to help us optimize some of the programming that we want to do with Python. The way that it can do this is to add in a few powerful data structures along the way. what this does is makes it easier for us to efficiently compute the arrays and the matrices that we have, especially when one or both of these are considered multi-dimensional.

Then we have SciPy, or Scientific Python, which is going to come with NumPy in many cases. Often you can't get one to work well without the other because they share many features. When you are working with SciPy, you are able to gain that competitive edge even more than just using NumPy on its own. This happens when you try to enhance some of the useful functions for regression, minimization, and so much more.

The Pandas Library

The next library that we need to spend some time on when we are looking for help with one of our data analytics projects is going to be known as Pandas, or the Python Data Analysis Library. You will find that the name gives away why this library is so important, and why we need to spend some time working with this as well.

Pandas are going to be one of the tools that work with Python, and it is also open-sourced so you can download it and start working with it without any problems. It is going to provide us with some great and easy data structures to work with, and it has a lot of high-performance abilities that will help as well. In fact, you will find that the Pandas library is able to help us out with all of the different programming things that we want to do when it comes to finishing the data analysis.

You are able to work with this library in particular when you want to add in some new structures of data and some new tools to help with the data analysis. And you will find that this work regardless of the kind of project that you would like to complete. There are many industries and companies that are fond of working with this kind of library to help them with things like finance, social science, engineering, and statistics to name a few.

The best part about using this library is that it is adaptable, which helps us to get more work done. It also works with any kind of data that you were able to collect for it, including uncategorized, messy, unstructured, and incomplete data. Even once you have the data, this library is going to step in and help provide us with all of the tools that we need to slice, reshape, merge, and more all of the sets of data we have.

Pandas are going to come with a variety of features that makes it perfect for data science. Some of the best features that come with the Pandas library from Python will include:

The Matplotlib Library

When you are working with some of the visuals that are needed in data analysis, you will find that the matplotlib library is one of the best ones that you would like to work with. This helps you to really visualize and understand all of the information that you have collected and really helps you to figure out the relationships that are going to come up with your models. It is also going to make it more efficient to see how the insights are going to be worth your time.

Working with these visuals is going to be so important. Depending on the kind of data that is in your models and that you have been working with the whole time, you will find that these visuals are going to make it easier to see what information you have gathered, and how the different parts are going to work when you try to combine them together.

This is one of the areas where you will see that this library is going to be useful. It is basically going to be a 2D plotting library that you are able to use with Python, and it can really help us by producing figures that are publication quality in a lot of formats. You will also see that it can offer you a variety of interactive environments to work with that can handle many platforms based on your needs. This library can be used with scripts from Python, Jupyter, IPython, and more to help get things done.

This library is able to help with generating scatterplots, error charts, bar charts, power spectra, histograms, and plots to name a few. If you need to have some kind of chart or graph to go along with your data analysis, make sure to check out what the matplotlib option can do for you.

The Scikit-Learn Library

While we are on the topic, we need to spend a few minutes looking at the Scikit-Learn library and how well it is able to handle some of the machine learning and data analysis work that you want to do with

Python. This one is going to have a ton of algorithms that work well with machine learning and these algorithms can often fit under the idea of supervised and unsupervised machine learning problems that are low to medium scale. This means that there are a lot of potential uses and applications to make all of this work.

When you are working with the Python language, and working with the Scikit-Learn library to help out with some of the machine learning, you will find that the main emphasis that we are going to see will be on things like how easy it is to use, the performance of the model, a bit on the documentation, and the consistency that we are able to get to show up on the API.

The TensorFlow Library

We can also work with the library that is known as TensorFlow. This is actually considered one of the best libraries out there that works with Python and can handle the work that you want to do with data science. This is a library that was originally released by the Google Brain Team. It was written out mostly with the help of the C++ language, which is a bit different but it comes with some of the bindings in Python, so you will be able to still use the language that you have been learning without having to worry about it.

One of the best features that you will see with the TensorFlow library is that it is going to have a flexible architecture that is nice for allowing the programmer to deploy it with one or more GPU's or CPUs on your device whether that is a server, a mobile, or a desktop device. And you can do all of this with the same API the whole time.

The Keras Library

Keras is going to be an open-sourced library form Python that is able to help you to build up your own neural networks, at a high level of the interface. It is going to be pretty minimalistic, which makes it easier to work with, and the coding on this library is going to be simple and straightforward, while still adding in some of the high-level extensibility that you need. It is going to work either TensorFlow or Theano along with CNTK as the backend to make this work better. We can remember that the API that comes with Keras is designed for humans to use, rather than humans, which makes it easier to use and puts the experience of the user right in front.

Keras is going to work with all of the best-known practices at the time when it is necessary to reduce the cognitive load. This Python library is going to offer us a consistent and simple API that will help us to minimize how many actions that the user has to do for the different parts of the code that are common, and it also helps to provide feedback that is actionable and clear if you do end up with an error on the code.

The Theano Library

Theano is another great library to work with during data science, and it is often seen as one of the highly-rated libraries to get this work done. In this library, you will get the benefit of defining, optimizing, and then evaluating many different types of mathematical expressions that come with multi-dimensional arrays in an efficient manner. This library is able to use lots of GPUs and perform symbolic differentiation in a more efficient manner.

Theano is a great library to learn how to use, but it does come with a learning curve that is pretty steep, especially for most of the people who have learned how to work with Python because declaring the variables and building up some of the functions that you want to work with will be quite a bit different from the premises that you learn in Python.

However, this doesn't mean that the process is impossible. It just means that you need to take a bit longer to learn how to make this happen. With some good tutorials and examples, it is possible for someone who is brand new to Theano to get this coding all done. Many great libraries that come with Python, including Padas and NumPy, will be able to make this a bit easier as well.

Inheritances to Clean Up the Code

In the general sense of things, inheritance is a tool that allows users to define a class, which derives all its functionality from a parent class while providing insight to add more.

Inheritance forms a core part of object programming because of how it can extend the functionality of an already existing class by introducing new features. It can be compared to a real-world situation of a birthright in which children inherit the properties of their parents in addition to the ones they already possess. The children may also derive a surname (the last name) from their parents. The inheritance serves as one of the four core concepts object-oriented programming (OOP), including polymorphism, abstraction, and encapsulation. Inheritance is a robust tool in the hands of programmers, allowing them to create and enable new classes to inherit or receive every one of the methods and properties of an already existing class or classes. As we have come to know, class refers to a template or blueprint of an object. As such, every object was created using a class, while the concept of inheritance comes in to devise a form of relationship between the blueprints. This property is a feature of object-oriented programming that is applied in defining a new class containing little to no modification to an already existing class. While the class from which the other class is obtained is known as the parent class or base class, the created class is regarded as the child class or derived class. The formation of the derived class involves the use of the base class, as well as some other added features. The general purpose of the concept of inheritance is to help improve code reusability.

The function of inheritance in object-oriented programming:

By making use of the inheritance feature, users can find it possible to have a blueprint that has the same attributes as the initial one.

How an Inheritance is Implemented in Python

To introduce inheritance into a code sample, you could use the following syntax:

class ParentClass:

 Parent class attributes

 Parent class methods

class ChildClass(ParentClass):

 Child class attributes

 Child class methods

Automatically, inheritance introduces reusability to a block of code because the child class comprises of everything found in the base class.

Methods of interaction between a parent and child class

When programmers make use of a concept in object-oriented programming like inheritance, they create interactions between parent and child classes in three main ways. They include:

Anything performed on the child class modifies a corresponding action performed on the parent class.

Actions carried out on the child class override the subsequent actions carried out on the parent class.

Actions performed on the child class are simple actions performed on the parent class.

Sample code for Python inheritance

To improve your understanding of the concept of inheritance and its application, let us consider some samples below:

We start by creating a base or parent class, with a child or derived class vehicle.

```python
class Taxi:

def __init__(self, model, capacity, variant):

self.__model = model    # __model is private to Taxi class

self.__capacity = capacity

self.__variant = variant

defgetModel(self):        # getmodel() is accessible outside the class

    return self.__model

defgetCapacity(self):        # getCapacity() function is accessible to class
Vehicle

    return self.__capacity

defsetCapacity(self, capacity): # setCapacity() is accessible outside the
class

self.__capacity = capacity

defgetVariant(self):        # getVariant() function is accessible to class
Vehicle

    return self.__variant

defsetVariant(self, variant): # setVariant() is accessible outside the class

self.__variant = variant

class Vehicle(Taxi):

def __init__(self, model, capacity, variant, color):

    # call parent constructor to set model and color

    super().__init__(model, capacity, variant)

self.__color = color

defvehicleInfo(self):
```

```
    return self.getModel() + " " + self.getVariant() + " in " +
self.__color + " with " + self.getCapacity() + " seats"
```

In method getInfo we can call getmodel(), getCapacity() as they are

accessible in the child class through inheritance

v1 = Vehicle("i20 Active", "4", "SX", "Bronze")

print(v1.vehicleInfo())

print(v1.getModel()) # Vehicle has no method getModel() but it is accessible via Vehicle class

v2 = Vehicle("Fortuner", "7", "MT2755", "White")

print(v2.vehicleInfo())

print(v2.getModel()) # Vehicle has no method getModel() but it is accessible via Vehicle class

Take note that the getName() method used in the sample code for the vehicle class is unspecified. The reason is linked to the fact that the vehicle class receives it from its parent class.

So, when the sample code is executed, the result will be the following:

output

i20 Active SX in Bronze with 4 seats

i20 Active

Fortuner MT2755 in White with 7 seats

Fortuner

The UML Diagram of Python Inheritance

To provide more clarity on this subject, take a look at the UML diagram outlined below. The diagram is connected to the sample code used.

The Super() Method:

What is the function of the super() method in Python?

The super() method enables users to gain access to the inherited methods which cascade into a class object. In the samples shown earlier, the super() method was used within the constructor of the derived class <Vehicle>. At this point, the super() method invokes the function of the parent class <Taxi>.

How the super() method is implemented

Assume that you are required to involve a method in the parent class, for example, vehicleinfo(), that is defined in the derived class. To do this, you can make use of the line of code showed below:

super().vehicleInfo()

In the same vein, it is possible to income the parent class constructor from the sub or child class __init__ making use of the command below:

super().__init__()

Implicit inheritance in Python:

Implicit actions happen in Python inheritance whenever a programmer defines a function within the base class alone. This type of inheritance is depicted in syntax using the simple sample shown below:

class super (object) :

def implicit(self) :

    print ("Super-Class with Implicit function")

class sub(super) :

  pass

su = super()

sb = sub()

su.implicit()

sb.implicit()

The output produced is as follows::

Super-Class with Implicit function

Super-Class with Implicit function

From a general overview, it can be seen that Python inheritance contributes immensely to object-oriented programming. As a result, it is of utter importance that you understand how inheritance works in Python owing to the object-oriented design of the language.

Reading and writing data

How to Read and Write Data in Text Format

Python is considered a powerful programming language for manipulating text files because of its simple syntax to interact directly with the files, features such as tuple packing/unpacking, and well-built data structures.

There are numerous functions present in pandas library to perform read operation on tabular data. Here is a table listing some of the functions.

Function name	Description of the function
read_csv	It is used to load the data from a file or a URL using a delimiter. It uses comma as the default delimiter.
read_table	It is used to load the data from a file or a URL using a delimiter. It uses tab as the default delimiter.
read_fwf	It is used to read the data, which is present in a fixed width column format having no delimiters in it.
read_clipboard	It is a similar version of data_table. But it doesn't read the data from files and uses the clipboard data for reading purpose. Thus, it comes handy to convert tables present in webpages.

Let us see an overview about how to use the above functions for converting the text file's data into a DataFrame. Here are the options under which the above functions fall:

Date-time parsing: It covers the combining power to combine date and time data present in numerous columns into one sole column while showing the result.

Indexing: It has the capability to use one as well as more than one column while returning the DataFrame. It also has the option to choose or not to choose the column names present in the file.

Iteration: It has the capability to support iteration of a large amount of data present in the large size files.

Data conversion and type inference: It covers personalized list for the value markers, which are not present and conversions related to user defined values.

Skipping data: It includes row, footer, and numeric data skipping from the file.

The most important feature for any function is type inference. By using it, we you don't need to worry about describing the column type like integer, string, boolean, numeric, etc. Let us see one example of csv file (comma separated values).

Let's see an example:

In [154]: !cat chapter05/csvExample1.csv

w, x, y, z, word

10, 20, 30, 40, this

50, 60, 70, 80, is

90, 100, 110, 120, fun

As it is a csv file, we can use the comma as a delimiter and use read_csv function to read the file into a DataFrame.

In [155]: df = pd.read_csv('chapter05/csvExample1.csv')

In [156]: df

Out [156]:

wxyzword

0 10203040   this

1 50 60 70 80   is

2 90 100 110 120 fun

It can also be done using the read_table function by describing the delimiter.

In [157]: pd.read_table('chapter05/csvExample1.csv', sep=',')

Out [157]:

wxyzword

0 10203040   this

1 50 60 70 80   is

2 90 100 110 120 fun

Note: We have used the cat shell command for printing the contents present in the file. If you are using Unix, and instead using Windows, you need to use the keyword "type" and not "cat" to print it on your screen.

It's not necessary that every file will have a header row. Let's see the below example:

In [158]: !cat chapter05/csvExample2.csv

10, 20, 30, 40, this

50, 60, 70, 80, is

90, 100, 110, 120, fun

We have two options to read this. One is to permit the pandas library to automatically assign the default column names. The other option is to specify the column names on your own.

In [159]: pd.read_csv('chapter05/csvExample2.csv', header = None)

Out [159]:

X.1X.2X.3X.4X.5

0   10203040   this

1   50   60 70 80   is

2   90 100 110 120 fun

In [160]: pd.read_csv('chapter05/csvExample2.csv', names = ['w', 'x', 'y', 'z', 'word'])

Out [160]:

wxyzword

0   10203040   this

1   50   60 70 80   is

2   90 100 110 120 fun

If you want to arrange the values in a hierarchy using multiple columns, you can pass the list of column names or numbers. Here is an example:

In [161]: !cat chapter05/csvExample3.csv

firstKey, secondKey, firstValue, secondValue

one, w, 10, 20

one, x, 30, 40

one, y, 50, 60

one, z, 70, 80

two, w, 90, 100

two, x, 110, 120

two, y, 130, 140

two, z, 150, 160

In [162]: parse_data = pd.read_csv(' chapter05/csvExample3.csv', index_col=[' firstKey ', ' secondKey '])

In [163]: parse_data

Out [163]:

firstValuesecondValue

firstKey secondKey

onew 10 20

x 30 40

y 50 60

z 70 80

two w 90 100

x 110 120

y 130 140

z 150 160

Parser function provides a lot of additional arguments, which can be used to handle many file format exceptions. For example, skiprows allows you to skip any rows present in the text file. Let's see an example:

In [164]: !cat chapter05/csvExample4.csv

Hi!

We are making it a little bit difficult for you

w, x, y, z, word

In today's modern world, you can easily skip any rows present in a file

10, 20, 30, 40, this

50, 60, 70, 80, is

90, 100, 110, 120, fun

In [165]: pd.read_csv(' chapter05/csvExample4.csv', skiprows = [0, 1, 3])

Out [165]:

wxyzword

0   10203040   this

1   50   60   70   80   is

2   90   100 110 120 fun

A very important part in the parsing process, which is commonly used, is "Missing data handling". In these cases, either the missing data is not present in the file or it is marked as a sentinel value. In parsing, pandas use common sentinels like NA, NULL, and -1.

Now let us see an example:

In [166]: !cat chapter05/csvExample5.csv

anyValue , w, x, y, z, word

one, 10, 20, 30, 40, NA

NA, 50, 60 , , 80, is

three, NA, 100, 110, 120, fun

In [167]: final_result = pd.read_csv('chapter05/csvExample5.csv')

In [168]: final_result

Out [168]:

anyValue w x y z word

0 one 10 20 30 40 NaN

1 NaN 50 60 NaN 80 is

2 three NaN 100 110 120 fun

In [169]: pd.isnull(final_result)

Out [169]:

anyValue w x y z word

0 F alse Fal se Fa lse F alse F alse True

1 True False Fa lse True False F alse

2 False True False Fa lse F alse Fa lse

The option na_values will either take a set of string values or a list while considering the missing values in the text file.

In [170]: final_result = pd.read_csv(' chapter05/csvExample5.csv', na_values = ['NULL'])

In [171]: final_result

Out [171]:

anyValue w x y z word

0 one 10 20 30 40 NaN

1 NaN 50 60 NaN 80 is

2 three NaN 100 110 120 fun

We can specify fifferent NA sentinels for every column present in the text file.

Now let's see an example:

In [172]: sentinels = { 'word': ['fun', 'NA'], 'anyValue': ['one'] }

In [173]: pd.read_csv(chapter05/csvExample5.csv', na_values=sentinels)

Out [173]:

something a b c d message

anyValue w x y z word

0 NaN 10 20 30 40 NaN

1 NaN 50 60 NaN 80 is

2 three NaN 100 110 120 NaN

Argument name	Description of the argument
Path	It is a string value that is used to indicate the location of file, file-like objects, or the URL.
Delimiter or sep	It is used to split the columns present in each row by either using a regular expression or a character sequence.
Names	It is used to show the result in form of column names, combined with the header value as None.
na_values	It is used to provide the sequence of values, which needs to be replaced by NA
Header	It is used to provide the row number that will be used as column names. The default value is 0 and is None in case there is no header row present in the file.

comment	It is used to split the character(s) comments after the end of lines.
date_parser	It is used for parsing dates from a text file.
index_col	It is used to provide the column names or numbers that need to be used as row index in result.
Nrows	It I used to pass the number of rows, which need to be read from the starting point of the file.
Verbose	It is used to print different output information, such as total number of missing values that are present in non-numeric columns.
Iterator	It is used to return the TextParser object to read the file in steps.
convertors	It is used to perform name mapping on functions.
skip_footer	It is used to provide the number of lines, which needs to be ignored at the end of the file.
Squeeze	It is used to return a series if the parsed data has only one column present in it.
chunksize	It is used to iterate and provide size of the file chunks.
encoding	It is used to provide the text encoding for Unicode system.
Dayfirst	It is used to deal with international format when ambiguous dates are getting parsed. Its default value is false.

How to Read Small Pieces of Text Files

We will have to read the file in small pieces of rows instead of reading the complete file. It can be done using "nrows".

In [176]: pd.read_csv('chapter05/example6.csv', nrows = 10)

Out [176]:

wxyzword

0 10203040   A

1 50 60 70 80   B

2 90 100 110 120 C

3130140150160D

4170180190200E

510203040F

650607080G

790100110120H

8130140150160I

9170180190200J

In order to read the file, we can also use chunksize for number of rows.

In [177]: file_chunker = pd.read_csv('chapter05/example6.csv', chunksize = 500)

In [178]: file_chunker

Out [178]: <pandas.io.parsers.TextParser at 0x8398150>

TextParser object gets returned from read_csv will be iterating the file as per the chunksize fixed above i.e. 500. Therefore, we can aggregate the total value counts in "key" column by iterating the example6 file.

```
file_chunker = pd.read_csv('chapter05/example6.csv', chunksize = 500)

total = Series( [] )

for data_piece in file_chunker:

total = total.add( data_piece[ 'key' ].value_counts(), fill_value = 0 )

total = total.order(ascending = False)

# Now we will get the below result:

In [ 179 ]: total[:10]

Out [ 179 ]:

F 460

Y 452

J 445

P 438

R 429

N 417

K 407

V 400

B 391

D 387
```

TextParser also has a get_chunk method. It helps us to read the pieces of random size from the file.

The Different Types of Data We Can Work With

The information that is processed in computer programs is represented in various ways. If you treat numerical information, you will use simple or real values or simple data. If you work logical expressions with true or false results you will use logical or Boolean data. If, on the other hand, you manipulate text you will use data of type character or string of characters (string). To represent numerical information (or even logical or text) where the data is grouped in the form of tables, such as vectors and matrices, or more complex structures, composite data types will be used.

The types of data used in the main programming languages are shown in the figure below.

Note: The character data type does not exist in Python, a simple character is represented as a character string (string).

Structures composed of languages such as C, FORTRAN, Pascal, Matlab, etc. Py: Composite structures in Python. Source: self-made.

Simple data

The elementary data is simple, also called scalars because they are indivisible objects. Simple data are characterized by having a single value associated and are of the integer, real or floating-point (float), Boolean and character type. In Python, there is no simple character data type. Although the data consists of only one letter or ASCII character it is represented as a data composed of a string of characters (string).

Integers

In mathematics, the integers are the natural numbers, their negatives and zero. Examples of integers: 5, -20, 0, -104. Numbers with decimal parts are not included among the integers, such as 3.4. Integers, in most programming languages including Python, are defined with the word int. Python has an internal type function that returns the given data type:

In C ++ or Pascal 4 bytes (32 bits are used, and one bit is reserved for the sign, signed 32-bit) for standard integers (int, integer), represented in the number range:

–2147483648... 2147483647

For greater range in these languages, 8 bytes (signed 64-bit) are used, declaring them as long or int64:

–263.......263 –1

Unlike C++ or Pascal, in Python integer data is stored with "arbitrary precision", that is, the number of bytes needed to represent the integer is used. For example, the numbers 5 (binary: 101) and 200 (27 + 26 + 23, binary: 11001000) are represented:

The internal Python bin (N) function converts an integer to string with the equivalent binary (0b + binary). To check the wide range of values in Python, let's test a value greater than 263, such as 2220

```
>>> 2**220

1684996666696914987166688442938726917102321526408785780068
975640576
```

Real

Unlike integers that are discrete values from one natural number to another, the continuous value numbers of the set of real numbers in Mathematics are called real or floating-point/point8, or simply float. Not all real numbers can be accurately represented in computer science because many have infinite decimal places. However, according to the level of precision, we want these numbers can be approximated well enough. The use of the IEEE 754 standard to represent real or floating-point numbers has been agreed for several decades, using scientific notation.

This notation allows you to represent numbers with a mantissa (significant digits) and an exponent separated by the letter 'e' or 'E'. For example, the number 4000 is represented by the mantissa 4 and the exponent 3, 4e3. It reads 4 times from 10 to 3. The number 0.25 is also represented as 25e-2. It is also allowed to omit the initial zero, .25 and the real number 4.0 can be entered as 4. (without the zero after the period).

Sign	Exponent	Mantista
1 Bit	11 Bits	52 Bits

Value= (-1)sign * 1.Mantisa * 2(Exponent-1023)

Thus, with 64 bits the numbers (decimals) of $\pm$ 5.0 * 10-324 (precision) can be represented up to $\pm$ 1.7 * 10308 range. The IEEE 754 standard updated in 2008 incorporates the decimal64 format that uses the decimal base to improve binary representation errors. Python incorporates the Decimal function of the decimal module.

Below are several examples of real numbers, the real type (float) and a typical error with representation of floating point with binary base, in the case of the value 0.1.

```
>>> 25e-2

0.25

>>> 4e3

4000.0

>>> type (4.)

<class 'float'>
```

```
>>> .2e2

20.0

>>> 1.1 + 2. 2 # is represented with binary floating
point error

3.3000000000000003
```

Booleans

The type of data to represent logical or Boolean values in Python is bool, in Pascal and C++ they are defined as boolean and bool, respectively. Boolean data takes the value True (1 logical) or False (0 logical). The Boolean name is used after George Boole, an English mathematician, proposed in the 19th century an algebraic system based on these two logical values and three logical operations: "and logical", "or logical" and negation. Examples:

```
>>> a = 3 > 2

>>> a

True

>>> type(a)

<class 'bool'>

>>> 4 > 5

False
```

Character

The type of character data used in several programming languages is the scalar or indivisible element of the texts used in computer science.

The texts are called a character string. For example, the ASCII characters ordered from decimal value 20 to 127 are:

```
! " # $ % & ' ( ) * +, -. / 0 1 2 3 4 5 6 7 8 9:; < =
> ? @ A B

C D E F G H I J K L M N O P Q R S T U V W
X Y Z [ \] ^ _ ` a b c d

e f g h i j k l m n o p q r s t u v w x y z { | } ~
```

The order in which they are represented serves to evaluate which is greater than another, according to the numerical value in which they appear in the ASCII code. For example, 'b' is greater than 'a'.

The character type is not defined in Python. Simple characters are defined just like a text with a single letter, that is, as a string of characters (string).

```
>>> type('a')
<class 'str'>
```

It can be seen that the character 'a' in Python is of type string (str), although in other languages such as Pascal it would be of type character (char).

Composite or structured data

Composite or structured data includes data with elements of values of the same type or of different types, which are represented unified to be saved or processed.

Characterized string data: string

The string data type is the basic structure for handling text, which includes alphanumeric characters and other characters of the ASCII or

UTF-8 encoding. Strings in Python are defined in single (') or double ("") quotes. They can also be defined in triple quotes ("''" '') when multiple lines are thrown. For example,

```
>>> 'Hi'
'Hi'
>>> b = "Wooden house"
>>> type(b)
<class 'str'>
>>> type (15)
<class 'int'>
>>> type ('15')
<class 'str'>
```

The texts 'Hi' or "Wooden house" are of type string in general in all languages. The value 15 is an integer type number (int), however, the value '15' is a string (str). If quotes (") or single quotes (') are included within a string, they may give erroneous results when these characters are used to delimit the string. You can use the character that has not been used as a delimiter within the text:

```
>>> 'She said "Cute"'
'She said "Cute"'
>>> "He doesn't know"
"He doesn't know"
```

However, in these cases you can also use the backslash character (\)
that serves as an escape to add quotes or other actions within the
string:

```
>>> print ('He doesn\'t know I \"will
come\"')

He doesn't know I "will come"
```

The backslash character (called escape character) followed by n (\ n)
indicates jump to a new line. Multiple lines can be included in a string
using triple quotes "" "..." "". In this case, line ends are included. Jump
to a new line can be seen when they appear on the screen with the
internal print function ():

```
>>> print ('We change line \ new line')

We change line

New line

>>> "" "

Program:

Author:

Date:" ""

'\ n Program: \ n Author: \ n Date: \ n'
```

Variables and assignment action

In mathematics, variables are used to represent numerical values. A
character or text is used to represent them. In mathematical calculation,
a function of the type $y = f(x)$ involves two variables, x, and y.

In programming languages, it is usually required to remember or save the numerical, Boolean or text values to be used once or multiple times in the program. The variables have this task. In languages such as FORTRAN, C / C++ or Pascal, a variable is considered a container or place within the computer's RAM, with an associated name (identifier), where a value of a certain type is stored. By using computer programs, we can stick with this concept. However, in Python, the concept is somewhat different, since the variables are not a place of memory that contains a value but are associated, or refer to, a place of memory that contains that value. The values can be an integer, real, boolean, etc.

Expressions and sentences

Expressions are the mechanism to make calculations and consist of combinations of values and identifiers with operators. They can include variables, data, operators, parentheses and functions that return results.

Every expression has a value that is the result of evaluating it from left to right, considering the precedents. Examples of expressions:

```
>>> 1.5*3/2

2.25

>>> 1.2*x + 3 # The value of x in the previous
example is 10.0

15.0

>>> 3 > (3.1 + 2)/3

True
```

The sentences or instructions are the basic units of the programs (also called in the slang of the programmers, codes) that produces an action, such as assigning a value to a variable, displaying a result, etc. The Python interpreter executes each statement producing the given action.

```
>>> y = x/2 + 3
>>> print(y)
8.0
```

```
>>> 1.5*3/2
2.25
>>> print (_)
2.25
```

The first sentence in the box on the left calculates the expression x / 2 + 3 and the result assigns it to the variable y. The second statement shows the value of y. But, the expression in the box on the right 1.5 * 3/2, whose calculation is not assigned to any variable, its result is saved associated with a variable called "_".

Operators

The operators are the symbols that represent the calculation actions. In addition to classical mathematical operations, logical and relationship or comparison operators are used in programming. We can classify the operators of 3 types: arithmetic operators, logical or Boolean operators, and relational operators.

Arithmetic operators

Operation	Operator	Expression	Result type
Sum	+	a+b	Integer if a and b integers; real if any

			is real
Subtraction	-	a-b	Integer if a and b integers; real if any is real
Multiplication	*	a*b	Integer if a and b integers; real if any is real
Division, a ÷ b (integer)	/	a/b	Always real
Division, integer	//	a//b	Returns the whole part of the quotient a ÷ b
Module, rest	%	a%b	Returns the rest of the division a ÷ b
Exponentiation, ab	**	a**b	Integer if a and b integers; real if any is real

Examples:

```
>>> 14/4      # Integer Division
3.5
>>> 14 // 4   # Division, returns whole part of
dividing 14 by 4
3
>>> 14% 4     # Module, returns the rest of
dividing 14 by 4
```

2

Arithmetic operators that operate on a single operand are called unary: sign change operator - and identity + operator. For example, -4, +4, --4 equals 4.

The Importance of Data Visualization

Before we can finish off our own data analysis, we need to take some time to learn about data visualization and how we are able to utilize this for some of our needs. These visuals are amazing because they can take all of the data that we have collected and sorted through and analyzed from before and puts it into a format that we can read and understand. Visuals and graphs are a whole lot easier to look through and gain the main meaning from than reading through reports and spreadsheets, which is why these data visuals are going to be such an important part of this process. With this in mind, we are going to dive in and take a look at the data visualizations and what we are able to do with them.

The Background of Data Visualization

To start with, we need to understand that data visualization is just going to be the presentation of data in a graphical or a pictorial format. It is going to enable some decision-makers to look through the analytics that we did with all of our data, but it is done in a visual manner. This will help everyone involved grasp difficult concepts or identify some new patterns that are important. Moreover, we even have the chance to work with visualizations that are a bit more interactive, which helps us to take this concept a bit further. This helps us to use a lot of our modern technology in order to drill down into the charts and graphs to find more details and can help us to change the data we see interactively, and process it to meet our needs.

With that information in mind, it is time for us to look a bit at some of the histories that are possible with data visuals. The concept of using pictures and graphs to look through data and understand it a bit more has been around for centuries. For example, how many times did travelers and even those who have gone to war worked with maps to help them see what is going on and to figure out what they did next?

Visuals can help us to figure out what kind of business we are looking at, can help us to separate out things in a group, and can even help with making maps and working with things like temperatures and geographical features that we need as well. This is a big reason why we would want to work with these to help with our data visualization.

The technology that comes in our modern world has really lit a big fire under data visualization and how it works for our needs. Computers have made it possible to go through and process a huge amount of data, and we are able to do it at incredibly high speeds as well. Moreover, because of this, we can see that data visualizations is a big blend of art and science that is already having a large impact over the corporate landscape over the next few years.

There are a lot of ways that we are able to work with these data visuals, and taking the time to learn how to use them, and to learn all of the different ways that you can work with these to help you understand what data you are taking in and what it means for you, can make all of the difference in how well you can use your own data.

Why is Data Visualization so Important?

Now that we have had a chance to talk about data visualizations a bit, it is important to understand why this is something that is so important. Why can't we just go through the analysis and then understand the information that is there? There are many reasons why you should work with the data analysis and why it is such an important part of the process that you should focus on.

Data visualization is going to be one of the quick and easy methods that help to convey all of these concepts in an easy to understand manner.

Think about how much you are able to fit into one of these visuals. Even language barriers are not such a big deal because we know what is found in the data just by looking at the image. And we can use one image to tell us a lot about the process and the data that we are working with, something that could take up pages of complicated jargon to do when we work with it on a spreadsheet or another document. This is all possible and easy to work with when we work on extensions to the Python language, such as the Matplotlib library that we talked about before.

In addition to some of the topics that we learned above, there are a few other ways that we are able to work with data visualization. Some of these are going to include:

The data visuals are going to help us to figure out which areas in our business are more likely toned some improvement and some of our attention.

These data visuals are going to help us to clarify which factors are more likely to influence the behavior of other customers.

These data visuals are going to make it easier to understand which products should be placed in different locations.

When they are used in the proper manner, these data visuals are going to be able to help a company predict their volume of sales so that they can do other things inside of the business to reduce waste and make more money.

Moreover, these are just a few of the things that the data visuals are going to be able to do for us. Moreover, with all of the different options that we can choose when it comes to working with data visuals, from pie charts, bar graphs, and so much more. This helps us to handle any and all of the data that we want in a safe and secure manner, while really seeing what information is hidden inside of it.

How Can We Use Data Visualization?

The next thing that we need to look at here is how these visuals are being used in the first place. No matter how big the industry is, all businesses are working with data visualization to help them make more sense of their data overall. In addition, there are varieties of methods that can be used to help with this one. Some of the ways that companies are working with data visualizations include:

It can help them to comprehend the information they are working with much better. By using graphs for the information of the business, it is easier for these companies to see a large amount of data in a manner that is more cohesive and clear. Moreover, they can then draw better conclusions from that information. Moreover, because it is always a lot easier for the brain to analyze information in a format that is graphic, rather than looking through spreadsheets and other methods, businesses are able to address problems and even answer questions in a more timely manner.

How to Lay the Groundwork

Before you take some time to implement some new technology, there are a number of steps that all businesses need to be able to take. Not only do you need to have a nice solid grasp on the data at hand, but we also need to be able to understand our goals, needs, and the audience we are working with. Preparing your organization for the technology that has to come with these data visuals is going to require that we can do the following first:

We need to have a good understanding of the data that we want to visualize. This includes the size and how unique the values in the charts are going to be to one another.

We need to be able to determine what we would like to visualize and what information we are hoping to communicate when we pick out a chart or a graph to use.

We need to have a good understanding of our audience and then understand how this audience is going to process information in a visual manner.

We need to use some visuals that can convey the information in the best and the simplest form that we can so that our audience is able to understand what is going on.

Once you have been able to meet some of these needs about the data you are working with and the audience who you plan to consume your products, then it is time for us to get prepared for data we would like to work with. Big data is going to bring in new challenges to the work of visualization because we are able to see some of the larger volumes and the varieties that are there. Even some of the changes in the velocities are going to be important when we work here so we cannot forget all about this. In addition, the data that we will use can be generated in a much faster than we can analyze it and manage it in most cases.

We can then use this to help pinpoint some emerging trends that will show up in the data. Working on these kinds of visuals is a good idea because it will help us to find some of the trends that are in the market, and some of the business trends that are important. When we can find these, and we use them in the right way, it helps us to get the most out of our competition. Moreover, of course, this is a good way to affect your bottom line as well. It is easier to spot some of the outliers that would affect the quality of the product or some of the customer churn, and then you can address these issues before they turn into a bigger problem.

Identify some of the patterns and relationships that will show up. Even extensive amounts of data that may seem complicated to go through can make more sense when you present it in a graphical format. Moreover, you will find that businesses using this can find all of the parameters that are there and how much they will correlate with one another. You will find that a few of these are going to be obvious, and you may not need this data analysis to get it to work, but others are harder to find. The graphs and charts that you want to use can help the company focus on the best areas, the ones that are the most likely to influence their goals the most.

Finally, these visuals are going to be good at communicating the story to others. Once the business has been able to go through and uncover some new insights from these analytics, the next part of the process will include what we need in order to talk about these insights and show what they are to others. It is possible to work with charts and even some graphs and any of the some of the other representations that are impactful and fun to look at because it can engage and can help to get the message across as quickly as possible.

As we can see here, there are a lot of benefits to working with these visuals, and being able to add them to your data analysis is going to make a big difference overall. Companies in all industries are able to go through and work with some of the visuals to help them understand the data that they are analyzing in a manner that is easier than anything else is. You cannot go wrong adding in some of these visuals to your work and ensuring that you can fully understand what is going on in your data.

Indexing and selecting arrays

Generating Arrays

There are different ways of creating arrays. The examples above illustrate the simplest, by creating a sequence or a list in the form of an argument with the array() function. Below is an example:

>>> x = np.array([[5, 7, 9],[6, 8, 10]])

>>> x

array([[5, 7, 9],

[6, 8, 10]])

Other than the lists created, you can also create one or more tuples in the same manner as shown below using the array() function:

>>> x = np.array(((5, 7, 9),(6, 8, 10)))

>>> x

array([[5, 7, 9],

[6, 8, 10]])

Alternatively, you can also use the same procedure to create more than one tuple as shown below:

>>> x = np.array([(1, 4, 9), [2, 4, 6], (3, 6, 9)])

>>> x

array([[1, 4, 9],

[2, 4, 6],

[3, 6, 9]])

As you work with ndarrays, you will come across different types of data. Generally, you will be dealing with numerical values a lot, especially float and integer values. However, the NumPy library is built to support more than those two. The following are other data types that you will use in NumPy:

- bool_
- int_
- intc, intp, int8, int16
- uint8, uint16, uint32, uint64
- float_, float16, float32, float64
- complex64, complex128

Each of the NumPy numerical types mentioned above has a unique function used to call its value as shown below:

Input

float64(52)

Output

 52.0

Input

int8(52.0)

Output

52

Input

bool(52)

Output

True

Input

bool(0)

False

Input

bool(52.0)

True

Input

float(True)

1.0

Input

float(False)

0.0

Some of the functions might need a data type to complete the argument as shown below:

Input:

arrange (6, dtype=uint16)

Output:

array ([0, 1, 2, 3, 4, 5], dtype=uint16)

Before you create a multidimensional array, you must know how to create a vector as shown below:

a = arange(4)

a.dtype

dtype('int64')

array([0, 1, 2, 3])

a.shape

Output

(4,)

The vector outlined above has only four components. The value of the components is between 0 and 3.

To create a multidimensional array, you must know the shape of the array as shown below:

x = array([arange(2), arange(2)])

x

Output

array([[0, 1],

[0, 1]])

To determine the shape of the array, use the following function:

x.shape

Output

(2, 2)

The arrange() function has been used to build a 2 x 2 array.

You will come across situations where you need to choose only one aspect of an array and ignore the rest. Before you begin, create a 2 x 2 matrix as shown below:

a = array([[10,20],[30,40]])

a

Output

array([[10, 20],

[30, 40]])

From the array above, we are going to select an item. Keep in mind that the index numbers in NumPy always start from 0.

Input: a (0, 0)

Output:

10

Input: a (0, 10)

Output

20

Input: a (10, 0)

Output

30

Input: a (10, 10)

Output

40

From the example above, you can see how easy it is to select specific elements from an array. Given an array a, as above, we have the notation a(x, y) where x and y represent the indices of each object within the array, a.

From time to time you might come across character codes. It is important to know the data types associated with them as follows:

Character codeData type

bbool

ddouble precision float

Dcomplex

fsingle precision float

iinteger

Sstring

uunsigned integer

Uunicode

Vvoid

For example, a single precision floats array can be identified as shown below:

Input:

arrange (5, dtype='f')

Output:

array ([0, 1, 2, 3, 4], dtype=f;pat32)

Slicing and Indexing

You learned about slicing standard Python lists in the other books in this series. The same knowledge applies when slicing one-dimensional NumPy arrays. You will also learn how to flatten arrays. Flattening arrays simply means converting a multidimensional array into a one-dimensional array.

The ravel() function can manipulate the shape of an array as follows:

Input

b

Output

array([[[0, 1, 2, 3],

[4, 5, 6, 7]]])

Input

b.ravel ()

Output

array([0, 1, 2, 3, 4, 5, 6, 7])

The flatten() function performs the same task as ravel(). However, the difference is that in the flatten function, the array is allocated new memory.

It is possible to set the shape of a tuple without using the reshape() function. This is done as follows:

Input

b.shape = (3,4)

Input

b

Output

array

([[0, 1, 2, 3],

[4, 5, 6, 7],

[8, 9, 10, 11])

Transposition is a common procedure in linear algebra where you convert the rows into columns and columns into rows. Using the example above, we will have the following output:

Input

b.transpose = ()

Output:

array

([[0, 4, 8],

[1, 5, 9],

[2, 6, 10],

[3, 7, 11])

It is possible to stack an array by the depth, vertical alignment, or horizontal alignment. For this purpose, you will use the following functions:

- hstack()
- dstack()
- vstack()

For a horizontal stack, the ndarray tuple is as shown below:

Input:

hstack((a, b))

For a vertical stack, the ndarray tuple is as shown below:

Input:

vstack((a, b))

For a depth stack, the ndarray tuple is as shown below:

Input:

dstack((a, b))

Common Debugging Tools

When you are working on some of the codes you would like to write in Python, there are going to be some times when things go wrong. The code may not work the way you would like, and little issues and bugs can become a problem for you to handle. It is important to know more about which tools you can use to not only prevent these bugs along the way, but to make sure you can fix them if one does show up in the coding you try to do with Python.

The neat thing about working with Python is it comes with a lot of different debugging tools. This is going to make it easier to check up on the code you are doing and to ensure you can get it to work the way you would like. There are tools that allow you to work from the command line, as well as from the IDE, and even some analysis tools that are going to come in and help you prevent some of these bugs in the first place.

Debugging Your IDE

The IDE, or Integrated Development Environment, is a great place to start when it is time to start on your big project in Python. This is also an important place where we are going to work on the debugging process because it has direct interaction with some of the coding you do in Python.

Now, you will quickly notice that the debugging tools you can use for your IDE will vary depending on what kind of IDE you would like to use. The good news is they all are going to have the same kind of features to get the work done, including the steps of running the code, setting the breakpoints, and examining the variable.

There are a lot of options when it is time to work with the IDE you would like to use. Whether you choose to go with one that comes with Python to keep things easier and to just download everything at once or you plan to use the specialized version you can find, you will see that it is easier to find a debugging tool for your version just by doing a simple search. Many of them are going to come with a similar kind of workflow so you're able to pick out the one that is the best for your needs.

Options for Debugging

There are a lot of different debugging tools we can use in order to get started with this process in our program. Learning which ones can handle some of the work we want to do and can ensure our programs work in a smooth manner as we want is going to be important. Some of the different options you can choose when it is time to work on the debugging process in Python include:

Pdb: This works on all of the major operating systems. This is going to be seen as the standard library debugger. The neat thing is that it comes with the installations of Python you already have.

Pudb: This one is going to work with Mac OS X and Unix. This is a visual console-based and even a full-screen debugger that has been designed as a more comfortable replacement that we can use when compared to the option above.

HAP Python Remote Debugger: This is a debugger that works well with the Windows system. It is going to provide us with the ability to debug our system from a remote location.

Windpdb and Rpdb2: This one is going to work on Windows, Linux, and Unix: We will see this one as a more advanced Python debugger, with support for some of the smarter breakpoints, embedded debugging, encrypted communication, changes to the namespaces, and multiple threads. It is also faster than some of the other options.

Rpdb: This one will work with Unix, Mac OS X, and Windows: This is the predecessor to the option we just talked about above and it is going to improve some of the usability we see with pdbs and adds in some of the support needed to handle the remote debugging. It is also going to come with the ability to debug embedded scripts, post mortem of unhandled exceptions, and the ability to debug more than one thread at a time

JpyDbg: This one is going to work with Windows, VMS, Unix, OS/2, and Mac OS X. It is going to be both a JPYTHON and CPYTHON debugging framework that has been changed up so it works as well inside of Jedit as a standard Jedit plugin.

DDD: This one will work with the Unix operating system. It is going to be a graphical command-line debugger that will help us to handle some of the debugging we would like to get done in our code.

Pyclewn: This works well with Unix and Windows: This one is going to allow the programmer to use Vim as their front end to get the work done that they would like.

Pdb++: This one is going to work with Mac OS X, Windows, and Unix. This is going to be a kind of extension from the pdb module we saw with our standard library and it is meant to be compatible with the predecessor as much as possible. The good news is it is still going to introduce a number of new features to make the experience of debugging as easy as possible.

Python-pydebug: And finally, we are going to look at this debugger that works well with Unix, Mac OS X, and Windows. This is a set of debugging decorators that will respect the settings for Django within our coding. It will allow a user the ability to turn PDB into a function, inspect an object, work with a line profiler, and even to disassemble the function if needed.

Preventing the Bugs

Of course, one of the best things you can do for your own coding and your own program is to make sure none of those bugs get into the program in the first place. In the beginning, this is going to be hard and you may worry that your code is never going to work because you get a bug in it. But the more you practice and learn about these debugging tools, the easier it is going to be to avoid some of these bugs and to make sure the coding is going to work the way you would like.

Learning how to prevent some of these bugs, or at least keep them down to a minimum when you are first starting with your coding journey, can be important. So far, we have spent our time talking about some of the reactive tools out there for finding and fixing the bugs that do show up. But what if we were able to prevent these bugs from showing up in the first place?

This is where a number of analysis tools are going to come into play for us. Using these tools will give us a handle on where the code is going. One thing to keep in mind with this though is that your code may not always go to a good place like you want it to. Some of the tools you can use in order to pre-debug your code include:

Pylint: This is known as a linter because it can look over the code you have and then make some suggestions on the things you can improve on within that code.

Pycodestyle: This is a good tool to use because it will make some recommendations for you and about how you should format the code you want to work with. The idea with this one is that if your code can follow some of the standard conventions, then it is easier to have other Python programmers take a look at it and gain a better understanding in no time.

Flake8: This is going to be one of those tools you will want to use all of the time. It is going to come with both of the two features we talked about in one, along with a few other features as well. This makes it easier to have all of the tools you need to check the code and make sure it is working well.

Neural Network and What to Use for?

Regular deep neural networks commonly receive a single vector as an input and then transform it through a series of multiple hidden layers. Every hidden layer in regular deep neural networks, in fact, is made up of a collection of neurons in which every neuron is fully connected to all contained neurons from the previous layers. In addition, all neurons contained in a deep neural network are completely independent as they do not share any relations or connections.

The last fully-connected layer in regular deep neural networks is called the output layer and in every classification setting, this output layer represents the overall class score.

Due to these properties, regular deep neural nets are not capable of scaling to full images. For instance, in CIFAR-10, all images are sized as 32x32x3. This means that all CIFAR-10 images gave 3 color channels and that they are 32 wide and 32 inches high. This means that a single fully-connected neural network in a first regular neural net would have 32x32x3 or 3071 weights. This is an amount that is not manageable as those fully-connected structures are not capable of scaling to larger images.

In addition, you would want to have more similar neurons to quickly add-up more parameters. However, in this case of computer vision and other similar problems, using fully-connected neurons is wasteful as your parameters would lead to over-fitting of your model very quickly. Therefore, convolutional neural networks take advantage of the fact that their inputs consist of images for solving these kinds of deep learning problems.

Due to their structure, convolutional neural networks constrain the architecture of images in a much more sensible way. Unlike a regular deep neural network, the layers contained in the convolutional neural network are comprised of neurons that are arranged in three dimensions including depth, height, and width. For instance, the

CIFAR-10 input images are part of the input volume of all layers contained in a deep neural network and the volume comes with the dimensions of 32x32x3.

The neurons in these kinds of layers can be connected to only a small area of the layer before it, instead of all the layers being fully-connected like in regular deep neural networks. In addition, the output of the final layers for CIFAR-10 would come with dimensions of 1x1x10 as the end of convolutional neural networks architecture would have reduced the full image into a vector of class score arranging it just along the depth dimension.

To summarize, unlike the regular-three-layer deep neural networks, a ConvNet composes all its neurons in just three dimensions. In addition, each layer contained in convolutional neural network transforms the 3D input volume into a 3D output volume containing various neuron activations.

A convolutional neural network contains layers that all have a simple API resulting in 3D output volume that comes with a differentiable function that may or may not contain neural network parameters.

How Convolutional Neural Networks Work?

A convolutional neural network structure of ConvNet is normally used for various deep learning problems. As already mentioned, convolutional neural networks are used for object recognition, object segmentation, detection and computer vision due to their structure. Convolutional neural networks, in fact, learn directly from image data, so there is no need to perform manual feature extraction which is commonly required in regular deep neural networks.

The use of convolutional neural networks has become popular due to three main factors. The first of them is the structure of CNNs, which eliminates the need for performing manual data extraction as all data features are learned directly by the convolutional neural networks. The second reason for the increasing popularity of convolutional neural networks is that they produce amazing, state-of-art object recognition results. The third reason is that convolutional neural networks can be easily retained for many new object recognition tasks to help build other deep neural networks.

A CNN can contain hundreds of layers, which each learn automatically to detect many different features of an image data. In addition, filters are commonly applied to every training image at different resolutions, so the output of every convolved image is used as the input to the following convolutional layer.

Convolutional Neural Networks Applications

Convolutional neural networks are one of the main categories of deep neural networks which have proven to be very effective in numerous computer science areas like object recognition, object classification, and computer vision. ConvNets have been used for many years for distinguishing faces apart, identifying objects, powering vision in self-driving cars, and robots.

A ConvNet can easily recognize countless image scenes as well as suggest relevant captions. ConvNets are also able to identify everyday objects, animals or humans, as well. Lately, convolutional neural networks have also been used effectively in natural language processing problems like sentence classification.

Therefore, convolutional neural networks are one of the most important tools when it comes to machine learning and deep learning tasks. LeEnt was the very first convolutional neural network introduced that helped significantly propel the overall field of deep learning. This very first convolutional neural network was proposed by Yann LeCun back in 1988. It was primarily used for character recognition problems such as reading digits and codes.

Convolutional neural networks that are regularly used today for innumerable computer science tasks are very similar to this first convolutional neural network proposed back in 1988.

Just like today's convolutional neural networks, LeNet was used for many character recognition tasks. Just like in LeNet, the standard convolutional neural networks we use today come with four main operations including convolution, ReLU non-linearity activation functions, sub-sampling or pooling and classification of their fully-connected layers.

Stride and Padding

Secondly, after specifying the depth, you also must specify the stride that you slide over the filter. When you have a stride that is one, you must move one pixel at a time. When you have a stride that is two, you can move two pixels at a time, but this produces smaller volumes of output spatially. By default, stride value is one. However, you can have bigger strides in the case when you want to come across less overlap between your receptive fields, but, as already mentioned, this will result in having smaller feature maps as you are skipping over image locations.

In the case when you use bigger strides, but you want to maintain the same dimensionality, you must use padding that surrounds your input with zeros. You can either pad with the values on the edge or with zeros. Once you get the dimensionality of your feature map that matches your input, you can move onto adding pooling layers that padding is commonly used in convolutional neural networks when you want to preserve the size of your feature maps.

If you do not use padding, your feature maps will shrink at every layer. Adding zero-padding is times very convenient when you want to pad your input volume just with zeros all around the border.

This is called as zero-padding which is a hyperparameter. By using zero-padding, you can control the size of your output volumes.

You can easily compute the spatial size of your output volume as a simple function of your input volume size, the convolution layers receptive field size, the stride you applied and the amount of zero-padding you used in your convolutional neural network border.

Parameter Sharing

You can use a parameter sharing scheme in your convolutional layers to entirely control the number of used parameters. If you denoted a single two-dimensional slice of depth as your depth slice, you can constrain the neurons contained in every depth slice to use the same bias and weights. Using parameter sharing techniques, you will get a unique collection of weights, one of every depth slice, and you will get a unique collection of weights. Therefore, you can significantly reduce the number of parameters contained in the first layer of your ConvNet. Doing this step, all neurons in every depth slice of your ConvNet will use the same parameters.

In other words, during backpropagation, every neuron contained in the volume will automatically compute the gradient for all its weights.

However, these computed gradients will add up over every depth slice, so you get to update just a single collection of weights per depth slice.that all neurons contained in one depth slice will use the exact same weight vector. Therefore, when you forward pass of the convolutional layers in every depth slice, it is computed as a convolution of all neurons' weights alongside the input volume. This is the reason why we refer to the collection of weights we get as a kernel or a filter, which is convolved with your input.

However, there are a few cases in which this parameter sharing assumption, in fact, does not make any sense. This is commonly the case with many input images to a convolutional layer that come with certain centered structure, where you must learn different features depending on your image location.

For instance, when you have an input of several faces which have been centered in your image, you probably expect to get different hair-specific or eye-specific features that could be easily learned at many spatial locations. When this is the case, it is very common to just relax this parameter sharing scheme and simply use a locally-connected layer.

Matrix Multiplication

The convolution operation commonly performs those dot products between the local regions of the input and between the filters. In these cases, a common implementation technique of the convolutional layers is to take full advantage of this fact and to formulate the specific forward pass of the main convolutional layer representing it as one large matrix multiply.

Implementation of matrix multiplication is when the local areas of an input image are completely stretched out into different columns during an operation known as im2col. For instance, if you have an input of size 227x227x3 and you convolve it with a filter of size 11x11x3 at a stride of 4, you must take blocks of pixels in size 11x11x3 in the input and stretch every block into a column vector of size 363.

However, when you iterate this process in your input stride of 4, you get fifty-five locations along both weight and height that lead to an output matrix of x col in which every column contained in fact is a maximally stretched out receptive fields and where you have 3025 fields in total.

Conclusion

This is the last part of the book. Thank you for making it through to the end of this book, let's hope it was informative and able to provide you with all of the tools you need to achieve your goals whatever they may be.

The next step is to start learning how you are able to implement the basics of data science and Python into your own business as well. These are big buzzwords that have been flying around the world of business, no matter what industry the business is in, and many companies are ready to jump right in and see what this data science can do for them. But actually, taking some of the steps that are needed and learning how to work with the data life cycle and all of the different processes that we need with this can make a difference, and taking that first step can be hard. This guidebook has taken the time to look at all of these different parts to explore how a business can get started with data science for their own needs.

There are a lot of different parts that come with the data science life cycle, and while it may seem like more fun to just create the model and be done with it, all of these steps are going to be very important to the results that we are looking to get. We have to work through the collection of raw data, cleaning off and organizing the data that we have, learning what insights are there, figuring out the best model to work with and training and testing it, and then completing the analysis as well. We will take some time to discuss all of these parts and more as we worked through this guidebook and figure out the best way to make these works for us as well.

The data science process is going to provide you with a ton of benefits overall, and you are going to enjoy how it is going to be in order to use this information to learn more about your customers, about your competition and more, so you can increase your bottom line and see some results with your business. It may take some time, and often it may take some programming knowledge and more to get it done. But you will find that with the help of the Python coding language, and some of the machine learning that we have learned in this guidebook, you will be able to make this work for your needs.

Working with data science is something that all businesses are able to use to help them get ahead and really see some results in the process. But it is a process that takes time and is not always as easy to complete as we might hope. With the help of this guidebook, and some of the tools that we have learned inside, get ready to use Python data science for your needs. I hope this book helped you with whatever you were looking for.

CPSIA information can be obtained
at www.ICGtesting.com
Printed in the USA
LVHW050440100221
678895LV00007B/1301